DANCING IN THE DARK

DANCING IN THE DARK

A Survivor's Guide to the University

ANNE PIRRIE

NINI FANG

ELIZABETH O'BRIEN

Artwork
by
Geoffrey Baines

Tilosophy Press

First published in 2021 by Tilosophy Press

Layout, design and typesetting by Gerry Cambridge
e:gerry.cambridge@btinternet.com

Artwork copyright © Geoffrey Baines
Cover artwork copyright © Geoffrey Baines

Text copyright © Anne Pirrie, Nini Fang
& Elizabeth O'Brien 2021

ISBN: 978-1-3999-0091-1

Printed in Scotland by Love & Humphries
www.loveandprint.co.uk

Contents

The Dancers Inherit the Party

When I have talked for an hour I feel lousy—
Not so when I have danced for an hour:
The dancers inherit the party
While the talkers wear themselves out and sit
    in corners alone and glower.

Foreword

RECOVERING FROM THE Covid-19 pandemic offers unique opportunities to face up to a form of 'lockdown' that has afflicted us since long before the pandemic: the isolation that can so often haunt those who study and work in universities. That feeling of being 'locked down' by our expectations. Am I good enough? Will I ever get this PhD? Is there a vaccine against imposter syndrome? Can I really hack it as an academic? *What am I doing this for?* What is my research about anyhow? Why does everyone else seem to know what they are doing? What is Enlightenment? Why do I feel I am fumbling around in the dark?

We hope that the text before you will help you to explore what other people mean to us when we have been isolated from them for so long. Does unfamiliarity breed contempt or compassion? We want this little book to open up a space for thought on what it means to be 'at university', to work in the university, or simply just to be, as scholars, academics, researchers, teachers, demonstrators and all the other words we use to describe people who 'are' at university. How do we deal with the unfamiliar? How do we cope with not knowing where to begin, or how to go on? The book is an invitation to have a conversation. It might start as a conversation you have with yourself. (Talking to yourself can be useful.) Or it might lead you straight into a conversation with someone you hardly know. (That's what happened to us when we started out to write this little book.) Sometimes the people you call strangers are the very ones who can persuade you that you are not so strange after all. You might find yourself talking to people who have quite different interests. Your conversations might unravel in wavy and colourful lines. There you are, in a purple patch. You might want to dance. You may fall silent or need to retreat to a darkened room. We suggest you begin by eavesdropping on the conversation that unfolds among the authors of this little handbook. This is not the type of handbook that provides practical assistance. It is a handbook that you can hold in the palm of your hand, that place of boundless promise.

Anne Pirrie, Nini Fang and Elizabeth O'Brien

From the authors

THIS LITTLE BOOK started out as a book chapter. Before we knew what was happening, it leapt out of the shadows, jumped into a fast-flowing river, swam across and crawled out on the other side. There it gave itself a vigorous shake, like a dog mad with joy. Words like 'performativity' and 'governmentality' flew off its glossy coat. It ran off across the green grass (not greener, just green) to greet some friends, old and new. More on them later...

Dancing in the Dark celebrates the joy of encounters across lines of difference. Its authors come from very different backgrounds. They have interests that span the natural sciences, the humanities and the social sciences. The book addresses the insecurity, uncertainty and fears that attend having one's being in the university and considers these as virtues rather than as failings.

We offer this little book as a gift. We know it is in good hands (yours). We thought long and hard about the title. Setting out to 'reclaim the university' seems a little over-ambitious in retrospect. Yet talk of survival doesn't seem quite enough. We want you to thrive, to flourish, to have fun. We hope that this unorthodox handbook will enable you to claim the middle ground, flit between shadows and light, dance in the dark, and, more importantly, rekindle the passion, integrity and commitment that lie at the heart of your endeavours.

We would like to acknowledge the support of the Scottish Funding Council for this endeavour. We're grateful to Harriet Harris, Chaplain at the University of Edinburgh, for the care, interest and enthusiasm she has brought to the project, and for giving us houseroom in the Abundant Academy https://www.ed.ac.uk/chaplaincy/abundant-academy. Thank you to Geoffrey Baines for drawing out lines that help us to read between the lines; and to Gerry Cambridge for design and typesetting. Thank you to Áine Mahon, University College Dublin, Omar Kaissi, University of Edinburgh and Irwin Epstein of CUNY for helpful exchanges on 'shadows and light' in the contemporary university, and for their friendship, in all its guises. Thank you for the music, Kari Manum from the Faculty of Performing Arts at the University of Stavanger, Norway. Last but not least, a big thank you to Richard Smith of Durham University. Richard's work on the 'virtues of unknowing', his treatment of the 'quieter epistemic virtues such as intellectual modesty and diffidence', and especially his celebration of *unknowing* have been a source of continuing inspiration. Unknowing is that feeling of not knowing quite where you are when you begin. It is being able to recognise the inter-relationship between shadows and light. Richard observes that 'acquiring knowledge is often less important than learning how to live with our knowledge.'

There is, of course, no vaccine against the *know-ingness* that gives rise to the questions raised in the Foreword. But this little book might just help.

Pirrie, A. (2019) *Virtue and the Quiet Art of Scholarship: Reclaiming the University*.
London: Routledge.
Smith, R. (2016) The virtues of unknowing.
Journal of Philosophy of Education,
50 (2): 272-284.

It's crowded on the dance floor. We have let go of each other's hands, as this is not an occasion for partner dancing (at least not yet). We jostle for position, listening for each other as the rhythm enters our bodies. We bask in the play of shadows and light. (This will come back to haunt us, but not yet.) Gradually we are swayed into jouissance. We have moved beyond the realm of the predicate (cool, learned, informed, erudite, solemn, majestic, warlike, educative, grandiose, eloquent, seductive, dissolute, modest, angry) and embraced the ineffable. We have 'arrived' as they say—and yet we have gone nowhere. Freed from the constraints of performativity and style, the dancers inherit the party. They revel in the play of light and shadow, neither subject nor substantive.

'You do realise we have a bloody book to write', exclaimed Nini.

'I hadn't forgotten', replied Annie. 'I was just trying to get started. You'll recall that we agreed with Elizabeth that we would embark upon the verbal equivalent of a triptych, a set of three works that are hinged together vertically and intended to

out of linearity: into shadow and light

be appreciated together. I am gathering the material for the left-hand panel and attending to logistics.' As their theme was the interplay of shadows and light in academic inquiry and in the contemporary university, it seemed only fitting that Annie should consult a lighting designer. There's no harm in thinking ahead, she thought. Indeed, that seems to be the only type of thinking that is officially sanctioned in the contemporary university. It seems that we are increasingly governed by 'linear understandings of learning processes' that can be made explicit and subject to the relentless glare of monitoring and surveillance. The triptych will hang in a place of refuge, she explained—a university, perhaps—or in another large space more suited to the act of contemplation, the exercise of attention, a place for bearing witness—or praying. The lighting needs to be just right. We need to make the darkness visible without getting lost in it.

Some commentators have pointed out that in the context of higher education, 'the term "dark" does not connote badness or corruption'. The word 'darkness' is used to refer to aspects of higher education that 'may be dim, obscure or caught in a blind angle.' They explore how the 'there is' (*il y a*) of Levinas 'could be transferred to an

UNKNOWN UNFORMED UNEXPLAINED

analysis of the state of things in higher education'. For Levinas, the *il y a* is 'what remains after [the] imaginary destruction of everything … a presence, as the place where the bottom has dropped out of everything, an atmospheric density, a plenitude of the void, or the murmur of silence'. Yet it is the common figurative sense of darkness that prevails in the examples provided, 'as when the weight of all the things unsaid is felt in evaluations of a course programme, or when tensions between members of staff in a department can smear and blacken the everyday atmosphere'. These scenarios invoke the 'want of spiritual or intellectual sight, gloom, sorrow or distress' of the dictionary definition of darkness. Similarly, in respect of students' experience, the notion of darkness is often invoked to describe the 'experience of failure and letdown, when struggling with and withdrawing from difficult courses never completed; for half-formed ideas and crippled thoughts, full of passion and heart, but unfit for the academic genre of writing; and for interior imaginative wanderings that seldom see the light of day'. There is an element of judgement evident here that is at odds with the *il y a*, 'the impersonal "field of forces" of existing', the 'something that is neither subject nor substantive'. By driving the half-formed and crippled to the margins, some established critics of the contemporary university seem to have 'caught the darkness' in the conventional sense. Despite their best intentions, they appear to maintain allegiance to an enlightenment project. 'Passion and heart' are *de facto* 'deemed unfit for the academic genre of writing'. One of the aims of the merry dance among the co-authors of this little book is to challenge this particular form of governmentality, to restore passion and heart alongside reason to academic practice, to reclaim the shadows as an educative space. Perhaps we are dancing around the issue. But that is precisely the point. This handbook is part of a broader, subversive endeavour to consign 'knowingness' to the margins and to queer the notion of the 'academic genre of writing'.

'We need to find the right place to hang the finished work', said Annie to Nini and Elizabeth. Even in dark places there is room for community, refuge and enlightenment, and the university is no exception. In what follows, we challenge the binary between shadows and light—and in respect of form—between lightweight and gravitas. Our aim is to reinstate the shadows as a place of possibility and to reassure the reader that the entertainment of doubt is the heart of the educational project.

WE ATTEMPT TO reconceptualise the relationship between shadows and light from a psychoanalytic and educational perspective, and to reinstate the centrality of ethical relations among us as co-authors. For us this is the key to living a good life and moving beyond the shadows of the contemporary university.

In an essay entitled 'The Problem of Imaginary Agents', the sociologist Jonathan Hearn draws attention to 'the tendency to imbue names for large and complex processes with an imputed agency'. He cites neoliberalism as a case in point, as it is often invoked as 'the cause of some result we decry'. Yet as Hearn explains, the reality is rather more complex:

> For instance, if the university becomes more economistic in its cost/benefit calculations, this is an effect of neoliberalism. In some very general sense this may be true, but to substantiate the claim we would need to trace out actual efforts to affect institutional policies, and the wider environments shaping those actions.

Hearn cites the example of the Work Allocation Model (WAM), a mechanism for standardising the number of hours academics can claim for various

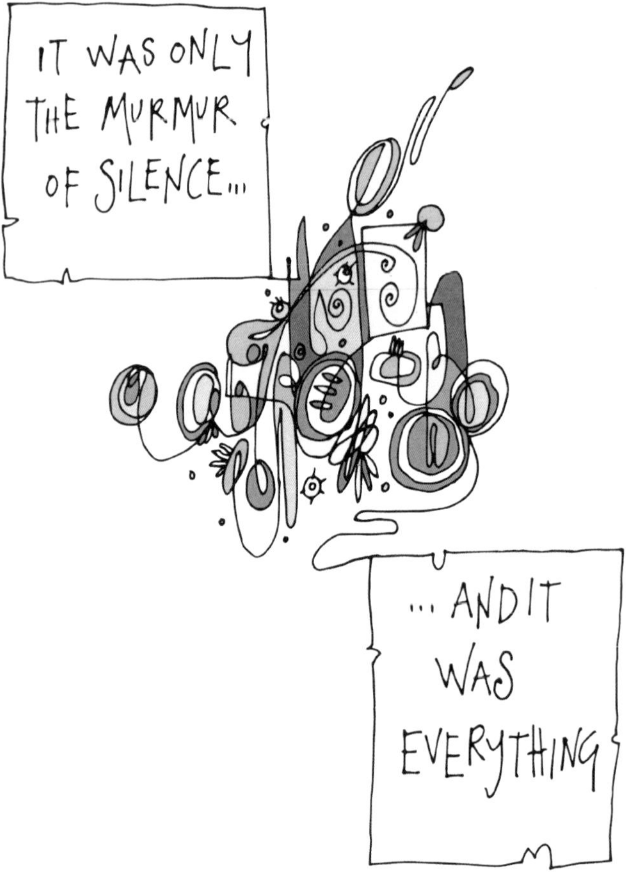
IT WAS ONLY THE MURMUR OF SILENCE...
... AND IT WAS EVERYTHING

activities. Elsewhere we have drawn attention to the damaging effects of this on the individual psyche. As Hearn points out, on the one hand the WAM 'is driven by managerial objectives of rationalising the allocation of university resources. But it is also driven by labour unions to ensure equity among staff for their work contributions.' Hence even at the systemic level in the university there is light in darkness and darkness in light. Neoliberalism casts a long shadow, despite the fact that it 'isn't a historical actor doing anything'. In this little book, we nimbly side-step these shadows, refusing to be oppressed by what Hearn describes as 'a dark "neo-liberal project" whose projectors remain unspecified'. We shall take each other by the hand and go visit Rainer Maria Rilke (1875–1926).

In *Letters to a Young Poet*, Rainer Maria Rilke offers advice to Franz Xaver Kappus, a nineteen-year old officer cadet who had asked him for his opinion of his poetry. The following passage invokes the 'atmospheric density', the 'plenitude of the void' and the 'murmur of silence' of the *il y a*:

> We have no reason to mistrust our world, for it is not against us … Perhaps everything terrible is in its deepest being something helpless that wants help from us…you must not be frightened if a sadness

rises up before you larger than you have ever seen; if a restiveness, like light and cloud shadows, passes over your hands and over all you do… Why do you want to shut out of your life any uneasiness, any miseries, or any depressions? *For after all, you do not know what work these conditions are doing inside you.* (our emphasis)

Rilke returns to the interplay between shadows and light in a poem that appeared in the Book of Hours: Love Poems to God. 'Go to the Limits of your Longing', he enjoins his readers. We are sent out into the world beyond recall, and the only way we can keep going is by 'letting everything happen [to us]: beauty and terror. No feeling is final.' What matters is that we do not lose sight of each other, even when we have no idea how or where we are going together, or how we are going to get it together.

Flare up like a flame
And make big shadows I can move in.

'Nini, thank goodness you're here', said Annie. 'I was beginning to feel the draft in this cavernous space, and the lighting director seems to have deserted me. I know that nearby is the country we call life, and that you will know it by its seriousness. Go make big shadows we can move in.'

*I*T's CROWDED ON *the dancefloor. Her hand now joined tightly with Annie's, Nini feels slightly queasy. She wonders whether Annie realises how uneasy she is at being here. Perhaps she can sense that unease through their physical contact. Nini clumsily pulls her hand away in an exaggerated movement that makes it look as though she is about to fall. She is afraid of her feelings being read by others, feelings that remain hidden even from herself. She can't tell if Annie has noticed anything as her face flickers in and out of the shadow. Do the dancers inherit the party? Nini isn't sure. Her pitch-black ponytail sways to her movement like that of a joyful Border Collie. The glaring light makes visible the mystery of her face. Her expression hovers between aloof grandeur and melancholy.*

What happened to the excitement that Nini felt when Annie and Elizabeth invited her to dance? 'Let's dance and let ourselves go!', they said. 'It's just dancing, not performing. You don't need to be good at it.' They knew she was not much of a dancer. Why did she feel so uneasy on the dance floor? What gave rise to the visceral impulse to retreat from her endearing companions? She could not make sense of it. Suddenly Nini realised that what she could bring to the party were psychoanalytic perspectives on the work darkness does inside us. Psychoanalysis (and education) are fields of study that address what eludes sense-making and cannot be readily understood. Paradoxically this process seems to be even less understood in education.

Psychoanalysis is a clinical practice that plays in the dark. Psychoanalysts, like dancers, think—but not in words. As Christopher Bollas points out, psychoanalytic thinking is less a cognitive or investigatory endeavour than an embodied process of intuitive, reflexive 'sensing'. This 'sensing' refers to the therapist's internal processing of what she notices and acknowledges at the bodily level: the sensory data and raw impressions that emerge when one is immersed in the lived world of another human being. These perceptual and sensory registers are welcomed by the therapist as having the potential to reveal the 'unthought known'. Bollas uses this term to refer to what is known at an experiential level yet at the same time remains in the shadows. The familiar strangeness of things, or rather, the strangely familiar. But, alas, words escape us. The unthought known dances in the dark, conjuring emotional

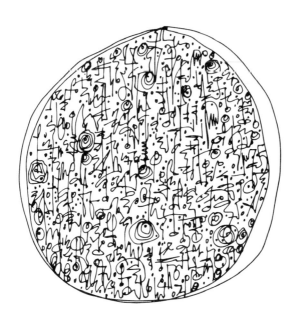

let us remember the world
is for us and shadows are
its gift

swirls that move us to think, act, perceive and relate to others and the surrounding world in ways that surprise us.

We make a case for the potential of psychoanalysis to help us to relish ambiguity and attend to the complex, dynamic tango between troubled knowledge in the personal sphere and the collective quest for knowledge in the educational sphere. We draw attention not only to the patches of dappled shade that reside in the unthought known, but also to the fact that this interplay between shadows and light is ultimately the source and condition of enlightenment. The light travels, passing through and reaching an object on its journey before casting a shadow that helps us see the depth of what has yet to be discovered (in psychic or educational terms).

The resistance to being fully known is tied to psychological disturbances that have occurred in response to relational difficulties, frustration and/ or deprivation. 'And yet', Elizabeth asks, 'bringing to light the unthought known surely also brings about the question of what it means to search for meaning in psychoanalysis?' 'How do we steer away from the obsolete portrayal of psychoanalysis in the popular media as the century-old paradigm that "couches" arbitrary, highly sexualised interpretations to address maddening neuroses?' asks Annie. Nini is encouraged by these questions, as they touch upon the fundamental issue of how we make ourselves available to be 'used' by the other, as Donald Winnicott suggested. In the clinical setting, this relates to how the therapist makes herself available to the client by letting her guard down, allowing emotions and impressions to arise freely in her. It is the therapist's emotionality that enables her to navigate the unlit realm of the client's unconscious world. The therapist, through attending to and sitting with a client, senses the feelings and internal disturbances aroused in her by the client. She endures this unsettling state of 'not-knowing-yet-experiencing'. Only then can she truly allow herself to come close to the silent agonies of the client and facilitate authentic dialogue. This is a place where old relational wounds may be revealed and explored in the present.

Nini stops here to tell Annie and Elizabeth about a particular incident from her clinical practice where she was accused of being selfish and uncaring by a long-term client after she had taken a three-week break. Nini recalled experiencing profound disturbance as the client launched into a relentless attack on her character. Being on the receiving end of the

listening to the
shadows and
hearing the
questions

client's chilling accusation, the battle between guilt and rage that Nini felt inside her made her doubt whether she and the client would survive the therapeutic journey. It was not theoretical sophistication, after all, but the entertainment of doubt that opened up space and prompted a search for beginning. She knew not to lose sight of the possibility that these feelings were themselves part of a much bigger story that needed to be heard. And that, perhaps, the client's acting out was her crying for help. The terrible dread persisted until her client burst into tears on hearing Nini say: 'I'm really not sure if what I am going to say is true, but I have a feeling that my being absent for three weeks has brought something back for you. There was a moment when I thought about your mother's leaving home when you most needed her as child…'

Learning from life implies being a willing participant in the often disturbing and infinitely complex mysteries of the mind: not knowing exactly what you are doing when you are about to begin; not feeling frightened of what you do not understand or what work the unthought known is doing inside you. In psychoanalysis as in education and indeed many other fields of human endeavour, reverence for what is unsaid yet palpably felt is what keeps alive the passion for truth, for human connection. At the time, Nini appreciated that Annie and Elizabeth took at face value her explanation of why she felt uneasy on the dancefloor. They accepted she was just feeling a bit light-headed and needed some fresh air. They did not pursue the matter further. They simply let her be. At the heart of relational ethics is a deep respect for each other's feelings of known and unknown origins as entities in their own right, while affording ample scope to think about the origins of such private terror when the other is ready for such engagement. This requires refraining from imposing premature assumptions about the other, as well as not being complicit in avoiding going to uncomfortable places with the other for the sake of personal safety.

Unobtrusive yet sustained curiosity is the language of care. It is the light of the sky in mid-afternoon that gently illuminates each corner of the room. Complete darkness is too terrifying, while the penetrating heat from a concentrated beam of light is too intense. The former makes Nini think of the long, dark Scottish winters and an intense current of melancholy sends shivers down her spine. She thinks of somewhere far more remote, the sub-tropical land where she came from. Home?

She wonders if part of her remains there still. Nini needed Annie and Elizabeth to remain curious about what was going on 'for' her in order for her to sit with the more unsettling rumination of what was going on 'in' her. Winnicott reminds us that learning about oneself is 'a sophisticated game of hide-and-seek' in which 'it is a joy to be hidden but disaster not to be found'. The implications for education, and for engaging in any educational project, broadly conceived, are as follows. It is only through the maintenance of curiosity in the context of ethical relations that teachers and learners are able to go to the paradoxical limits of their longing, to hide and (not) be found. The hide-and-seek becomes a meeting place of shadows and light where students can 'be isolated without having to be insulated', where the present is intertwined with the past, where there is scope for self-revelation and self-concealment. There on the dancefloor, amongst the flickering lights, for a moment Nini thought she saw her mother's face when Annie's face faded in and out of the shadows. She thought she saw tears in her eyes. She felt sorry that she had to let her go in order to find herself. And with that she lets the image of her mother slip off into the shadows.

tarry
with me
awhile before you name me

You darkness whence I came,
I love you more than the light
which marks the world's seam
by her gleaming for some orbit,
apart from which
No one knows who she is.

But the darkness holds it all in:
figures and flames, beasts and me,
whatever it may catch,
human and rights—

It is possible that there might
be moving a power right next to me.

Thinking, in psychoanalysis, means coming into contact with what was previously unthought but of potential significance for the subject. As Bollas explains, 'I know that I am in the process of experiencing something, but I do not as yet know what it is, and I may have to sustain this not knowing for a long time'. From mysteries we derive the treasures of the mind, our passion for truth, creativity, and our connection with others. In darkness, we no longer see the links between the symptoms and the cause, between outward behaviour and explanation. The darkness dims our habitual seeing and leaves us with what is still there (*il y a*): the ineffable know-ing, the formlessness of unbound ideas and the 'inevitable, ever-present, and necessary uncertainty about why we feel as we do'. It is left to us to give to 'our private, ongoing consideration of [our feelings] a certain humility and responsibility'. Something of this is captured by Rilke in his simple affirmation of darkness: 'I believe in nights.'

THINKING ABOUT SHADOWS AND
LIGHT, DIFFERENTLY

'I BELIEVE IN nights, and in the value of shadows' affirmed Elizabeth, to nobody in particular. How can those engaged and interested in education think about light and shadow differently? Shadow is more than darkness and light is more than brilliance. She was thinking of the relief both shade and illumination can provide, how warm sunshine falling on a sturdy tree and the shadow it casts in response require and complement each other. It occurred to her that shadows are where we see light and life interact.

When the trio stepped off the dancefloor at Nini's request, they all recognised something in Nini that they could not see, not even Nini. Annie and Elizabeth knew that there were elements of their friend they would never fully know and that in order to *be* friends and colleagues, in order to dance together educatively, this essential unknowability was to be respected. Stanley Cavell writes that 'there are special problems about our knowledge of another… And these problems can be said to invoke a special concept of knowledge, or region of the

the deeper
your curiosity,
the larger
our world

concept of knowledge, one which is not a function of certainty'. They needed to find a way to be curious and to be spacious. In other words, they needed to ask different questions and to seek response in a more careful way.

Could philosophy (of education) help here? Philosophical thinking on questions and answers, shadow and light, contrasts distinctly with the standard pattern of the empirical. As psychoanalysis can help us attend to troubled knowledge, philosophy has the potential to help students and researchers attend to difficult questions. Philosophical approaches have particular ways of describing the value of not knowing. Cavell refers to how Wittgenstein approached the solving of problems not through the provision of new information but by arranging what we have always known. The questions philosophers of education engage with arise from reality, rather than interrogate it. They resist comprehensive treatment, holding a certain essential openness. Philosophical thinking and research approaches can exercise our attention, stretch it in new ways and excite a new appreciation for these resistant questions.

Characterised by open enquiry, 'good philosophy helps us to pursue these questions and pursue them where they lead'. Moving from light into shadow is one way of thinking about following a train of thought into a place of questions. It is not intuitive to seek a position where educators and their students see less clearly, but Simone Weil challenges the advantage clarity affords. Using reason 'makes things transparent to the mind', which does not make the problem clearer, but rather removes the dust from the window of our thinking. We see *through* that which is transparent. Seeking clarity may move the thinker on from their question, but in fact the clarity gained partly determines the lens through which they view the world. Gaining clarity in this way both allows one to see and changes how one sees. Weil warns that reason should be employed respectfully, that the view it provides is of 'the true undemonstrables, which are reality' rather than a vista that offers no questions. In this way, reason affords understanding that we might better appreciate and attend to the incomprehensible. Weil invites us to imagine vision and understanding in a new way, by being open to seeing while not understanding, and to the power of our attention.

What of an educative, appreciative attitude to not knowing? As children we are fearful of shadows. Darkness signals the end of the day and the

at the heart of it
was a most beautiful question

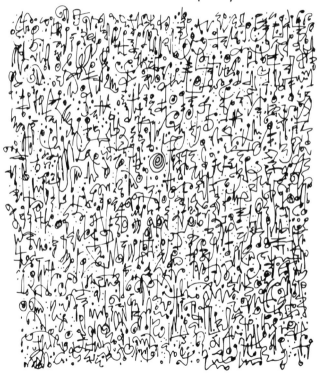

narrowing of our choices. It is a childish insistence to keep a light on so that we might always be able to see and know where we are. Over the years that fear becomes curiosity. The child finds a way to dispel darkness by suspending presuppositions and becoming interested. This attention-as-looking without attachment is Simone Weil's attentive light. In Weil's philosophy attentiveness is a suspension of thought and opening our minds to let another's thinking in. Encountering difference is a pleasure if one is attentive, and it makes clear how much more there is to know about the other person. Weil distinguishes between understanding and interpreting, similar to describing a philosophical approach to education from other empirical modes. The educational philosopher aspires to a 'method for understanding images, symbols, etc. Not to try to interpret them, but to look at them till the light suddenly dawns'. This is what Weil terms *attention*. The light is not in answering the question but in attending to it.

There are certain telling characteristics of Henri Matisse's *Dance 1*, the artwork that partly inspired this writing, which give a useful insight into the tension between what is seen and what is understood. Matisse is said to have described his approach as not painting things, but painting the difference between things. The dancers pictured are vibrant and dynamic, while inhabiting a well-defined space. They share a focus in forming a circle, yet the circle is incomplete. It is clear that they are dancing even though no two are moving in precisely the same way. Oriented towards each other, Matisse's dancers are in it together and free to be themselves. Finally, the name of the painting is important. Matisse's image of a group of people, atop a hill, against a background of blue sky or sea is not what he painted. He painted the dance. This dance is both effortless and clear; there is no question that Matisse might be depicting a regimented march (or a meeting), nor an unrestrained fit (or a pursuit without discipline).

It is difficult to resist the allure of strong definitions and final conclusions, of solutions and resolution. Matisse's *Dance 1* has been described as 'an image where form matches content', a painting which both visualises and communicates pure joy (https://www.henrimatisse.org/the-dance.jsp). There is a continuity between what the observer sees and what they understand, which is achieved by depicting neither. In education likewise what can be seen and what is done to achieve that which is seen is not the whole, nor, we would suggest, is it the

WE ARE LEARNING TO BE SURPRISED
NOT TRAINING AGAINST SURPRISE

point. Education, like the dance, is the name given to a recognisable and indefinable relation between the unthought known and those difficult questions. Embracing this openness makes education educative, distinguishing it from technicised schooling.

The language of not knowing calls for attention too. Words such as 'encroach' and 'retreat' are used to describe shadowy dynamics by those who would invite into their circle only that which they can grasp. There is an educational imperative to take care of language, taking responsibility for our words and their meaning, and to take care with language, acknowledging that we cannot fully know what our words will mean to others. In this careful approach there is the potential to value the shadow of the unknown other. An openness to the unknown through language is valuable in educational relationships. Think of the spacious and curious mindset Annie and Elizabeth reach for in order to appreciate their friend. Opening the circle, and holding its openness to be essential, moves the conversation on educative collaboration and community from integration to appreciation, to growing glad of difference.

Philosophy can help us to look at the shadows of education as the locus of difficult questions which resist attempts to be driven out into the empirical light. A philosophical approach allows the researcher to test and experiment with their thinking, as distinct from methodologies which purport to test the culmination of thought. In imagining an incomprehensible question to be reasoned out or another person fully understood the attitude shifts from attention to will, from the human to the technical. It is to become inattentive to the other by supposing to know them. Weil describes beautifully the consequences of such inattentiveness:

> What could be more stupid than to tighten up our muscles and set our jaws… Attention is something quite different. Pride is a tightening up of this kind. There is a lack of grace (we can give the word its double meaning here) in the proud man. It is the result of a mistake. Attention…presupposes faith and love.

Acknowledging the essential unknowability of the other embodies the curiosity Nini identified as necessary to thrive. It is a dwelling with the other person, attending to them fully, openly and without presumption. In acknowledging we appreciate each other and in doing so allow relation to appreciate.

There is, by our account, too great an insistence upon certainty, on shining light and chasing shadows. Too great an insistence that circles and inquiry be closed. We would like the space to dwell in the shadows of gathered questions and invite them into the gentle light of consideration. Matisse calls on us to attend to openness through *Dance 1* by leaving the circle incomplete. Without breaking the line of colour, he leaves a gap between the dancers' hands at the point closest to the observer. It is a moment of suspense and invitation, though invitation to what is not clear. The consistent colour has the obscuring effect of a shadow, one which holds a question. Can we attend to shadows, appreciate the unknown, hold the circle open?

Finally ➤

imagination and
reality dance
and play

sometimes
shrieking with
delight

Notes

'**linear understandings of learning processes**' Søren
Bengsten and Ronald Barnett (2017) Confronting the
dark side of higher education. *Journal of Philosophy of
Education,* 51(1), 114–131; see p.115.

'**the term "dark" does not connote badness or
corruption … caught in a blind angle**' ibid. p. 115.

'**there is' (il y a) of Levinas 'could be transferred
to an analysis of the state of things in higher
education**' ibid. p. 115.

'**what remains after [the] imaginary destruction
of everything**' Emanuel Levinas (1987) *Time and the
Other* (trans: R.A. Cohen). Pittsburgh, P.A. Duquesne
University Press.

'**as when the weight of all the things unsaid…**'
Bengsten and Barnett, p. 118.

'**experience of failure and letdown…**' ibid. p. 115.

'**the impersonal "field of forces" of existing', the
'something that is neither subject nor substantive**'
Levinas, pp. 46–47.

'**Passion and heart … the genre of academic writing**'
Bengsten and Barnett, p. 115.

'**the tendency to imbue names for large and complex
processes with an imputed agency**' Jonathan Hearn
(2020) 'The Problem of Imaginary Agents' https://bit.
ly/2JUGllH

Nini Fang, Elizabeth M. O'Brien and Anne Pirrie (2019). Care, contingency and capability: ecological perspectives on higher education. *Ars Educandi* https://czasopisma.bg.ug.edu.pl/index.php/arseducandi/article/view/3561

Rainer Maria Rilke (2004) [1929]. *Letters to a Young Poet* (trans: Herter Norton, M.D). New York: W.W. Norton.

'Go to the Limits of your Longing' Rainer Maria Rilke (1899[2001]) *The Book of Hours: Prayers to a Lowly God* (trans: A. S. Kidder). Evanston, Illinois: Northwestern University Press.

On psychoanalytic thinking: **'sensing'**, the **'unthought known'**: Christopher Bollas (2017) *The Shadow of the Object: Psychoanalysis of the Unthought Known.* London: Taylor & Francis Group, p. 139.

Donald Winnicott (1969) 'The Use of an Object', *International Journal of Psycho-Analysis*, 50: 711–716.

'not-knowing-yet-experiencing' Bollas, p. 136.

'a sophisticated game of hide-and-seek … a joy to be hidden but disaster not to be found'
Donald Winnicot (1965) 'Communicating and Not Communicating Leading to a Study of Certain Opposites' in *The Maturational Processes and the Facilitating Environment: Studies in the Theory of Emotional Development* (pp. 179–192). London: Hogarth, p. 187.

'You darkness whence I came…' Rainer Maria
Rilke, (1899[2001]) *The Book of Hours: Prayers to a
Lowly God* (trans: A. S. Kidder). Evanston, Illinois:
Northwestern University Press.

**'I know that I am in the process of experiencing
something…'** Bollas, p. 136.

**'the inevitable, ever-present, and necessary
uncertainty about why we feel as we do.'**
Ibid. p. 136.

'our private, ongoing consideration…'
Ibid. p. 136.

**'there are special problems about our knowledge
of another…'** Stanley Cavell (2002). *Must We Mean
What We Say? A Book of Essays* (Second Edition).
Cambridge: Cambridge University Press, p. 238.
Stanley Cavell (2012). Philosophy as Education. In
N. Saito & P. Standish (Eds.), *Stanley Cavell and
the Education of Grownups.* New York: Fordham
University Press.

**'good philosophy helps us to pursue these questions
and pursue them where they lead'** Paul Standish
(2010) What is the Philosophy of Education? In
R. Bailey (Ed.), *The Philosophy of Education: An
Introduction.* London: Continuum.

'makes things transparent to the mind' Simone Weil
(2002). *Gravity and Grace* (Second Edition). London:
Routledge, p. 132.

'the true undemonstrables, which are reality'
Ibid. p. 132.
'method for understanding images, symbols, etc.
Not to try to interpret them, but to look at them till
the light suddenly dawns' Ibid. p. 132.
'What could be more stupid than to tighten up our
muscles and set our jaws…' Ibid. p. 116–117.

Notes on the authors

Anne Pirrie is a Reader in Education at the University of the West of Scotland.

Nini Fang is a lecturer in Counselling and Psychotherapy at the University of Edinburgh.

Elizabeth O'Brien is a second- and third-level educator and a PhD candidate at University College Dublin.

Permissions

For the Reader...the subsequent seven pages
are left blank for your own dances,
jottings, considerations. Are you
ready to dance?

This book is set primarily in Minion Pro, a font
family designed by Robert Slimbach
and first released in 1990. Inspired by late
Renaissance typefaces, and available in
an extensive range of styles and weights,
suitable for a wide range of text applications
in numerous languages, Minion is a versatile,
stylish typeface which sets economically and
was famously used for the text of the
poet-typographer Robert Bringhurst's classic book
The Elements of Typographic Style.

Notes, subtitles & other matter are set in
Matthew Carter's rugged, slightly sculptural
Carter Sans which occupies an intriguing
middle ground between serif and sans serif.
Released for licence in January 2011 it is a 'hybrid
sans serif' with an unusually graceful italic.